ALLAN MORRISON 's books include *Haud Ma Chips, Ah've Drapped the Wean!*, *Should've Gone tae Specsavers, Ref!*, *Last Tram tae Auchenshuggle!* and *Kerryoans up the Clyde!* His media appearances include *The One Show* and *The Fred MacAulay Show*. He is involved in charity work and after-dinner speaking, and is a member of his local Rotary club. Allan enjoys hill-walking, sport and travel. He lives in the West of Scotland and he is the proud grandfather of four grandchildren.

By the same author

'Dinna Fash Yersel, Scotland!': Scottish Grannies' Sayings for Challenging Times, Luath Press, 2022

Kerryoans up the Clyde: It could only happen on the Waverley, Luath Press, 2021

'Haud That Bus!' The humorous adventures of Bus Pass Barbara & Bus Pass Molly, Luath Press, 2018

'Naw First Minister!', Luath Press, 2015

'Goanae No Dae That!': The best of the best of those cracking Scottish sayings!, Luath Press, 2014

'Should've Gone tae Specsavers, Ref!', Luath Press, 2013

'Haud Ma Chips, Ah've Drapped the Wean!': Glesca Grannies' Sayings, Patter and Advice, Luath Press, 2012

Last Tram tae Auchenshuggle!, Luath Press, 2011

'Haud ma teeth till Ah tie ma lace!'

Everyday banter overheard in Glasgow

ALLAN MORRISON

Illustrations by
BOB DEWAR

Luath Press Limited
EDINBURGH
www.luath.co.uk

First published 2024

ISBN: 978-1-80425-176-8

The author's right to be identified as author of this book
under the Copyright, Designs and Patents Act 1988 has been asserted.

This book is made of materials from well-managed,
FSC®-certified forests and other controlled sources.

Printed and bound by
Ashford Colour Press, Gosport

Typeset in Meta and Freight Text Pro by
Main Point Books, Edinburgh

© Allan Morrison 2024

With many thanks to Robin McAuslan.

Contents

Introduction	9
Juicy Patter Around Glasgow!	11
Buchanan Bus Station	13
Queen Street Railway Station	25
George Square	31
Buchanan Street	41
Sauchiehall Street	71
Argyle Street	93
Glasgow Subway	121
Central Station Concourse	127
Upper Hope Street	153

Introduction

'PEOPLE MAKE GLASGOW' is the brand name for Scotland's largest city.

The slogan could equally be 'People Make Glasgow Funny' with much of the hilarious everyday banter heard around the city. You see, Glasgow patter can be direct, unrestrained, loud, sometimes irreverent, but always juicy, entertaining and reflective of the quick wit and humour of the Weegie.

It's not polite to listen to other people's conversations, but sometimes in Glasgow it is compulsive as so many of them are hilarious.

Whether it's gossip about relationships, ageing, parenting, snobbery (aye, it exists in Glasgow, too!), money or sporadic outbreaks of maudlin sentiment, you will hear them delivered in the unique, robust, Glasgow cutting-edge-patois all over the city. In some instances, I have, shall we say, moderated the language used.

Listen, and you may unintentionally overhear gold nuggets of stonkingly creative remarks in the heart of this busy, beloved city. That is what the compiler of this book did along with the added assistance of a few friends, embarking on a listening survey over a period of months.

It's Glaswegian cool! So that's you telt!

Juicy Patter Around Glasgow!

Glasgow, the funniest, the warmest, the kindest and the hardest of cities. There's nothing quite like listening to Weegies chatting so it's been relatively easy to assimilate this collection of crackers in well-known city locations for one simple reason... Weegies talk rather loudly!

Buchanan Bus Station

Two young men standing at destination board

'Have you seen his new girlfriend fae Carntyne? Everybody says she's a bit of a stunner.'

'Aye. Probably works in an abattoir.'

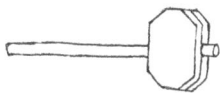

Two middle-aged women chatting in the bus station restaurant

'Aggressive? She's the type that would kill efter mating.'

Tourist approaches man in Buchanan Bus Station concourse

'Excuse me, sir. Can you tell me the way to Edinburgh, please?'

'Sure, mate. Jist get yer compass oot and walk east fur aboot 40 miles until ye meet some smug, well-heeled folks that ye cannae understaun' whit they're saying. Jist kidding, mate! The bus at stance 52 is fur Edinburgh.'

Two men standing waiting on a coach at stance 51

'See them that's staunin' ootside haudun' up notices, if ye ask me that lot jist come oot oan strike an' then decide whit fur efter.'

Two women standing at stance 56

'Posh! That wan wid take the rubbish oot tae her wheely bin in a suitcase.'

Two ladies gossiping standing beside Wincher's statue

'He went out to some clinic in Turkey to get new teeth and a partial hair transplant. Now half his teeth have apparently fallen out and so has most of the new hair.'

'Not much Turkish delight there, then!'

Two women talking beneath clock

'There's that very woman o'er there Ah wis talkin' aboot. Lost her husband over a year ago and still wears a lot of black. Knocks aboot like Morticia Addams.'

American tourist approaches bus driver who is standing beside his coach

'Excuse me, where would I get a bus to Hadrian's Wall?'

'Sorry, sir, but the last bus left aboot 2,000 years ago. Ye better ask at the enquiries kiosk.'

Elderly couple standing chatting to other passengers

'Somebuddy told me ye cannae even fart on these new zero-emission buses.'

Ladies blethering while waiting for coach to Glasgow Airport

'I was told she has Botox all the time. Probably couldnae smile even if she won the lottery.'

Young ladies chatting in queue for 901 to Largs

'My new medicine from the doctor is taking a while to kick in.'

'Then you should try your old one. Double vodkas and orange.'

Two women talking as they come off a West Coast Motors coach

'Glaikit wid be a compliment fur him.'

Two men just about to board their coach to Aberdeen

'Twisted doesnae come near it. Lady Macbeth without the sincerity, if you ask me.'

Two women chatting coming from bus stance 55

'Ah'm fair puckled still. Had to run to catch the bus in Baillieston. Ah waved tae the driver, lifted ma skirt up two inches an' he held oan fur me. Nice lookin' fella.'

Ladies sitting waiting for their bus to come into the stance

'She's been oan a diet fur months. Far too skinny noo. Doesnae even have enough room in her fur a wee watery fart.'

Two women talking about the cost of living while one is putting a letter in the bus station post box

'Ah jist told ma tribe, nae mair tins o' drink. We need tae cut back. If yer thirsty, there's plenty o' Cooncil juice in the tap.'

Well-dressed lady putting coins in mendicant's cup near Greggs outside Buchanan Bus Station

'Now, I hope this is for a hot meal.'

'Naw, hen. Ah'm savin' fur a Rolls. Ma Bentley's clapped oot.'

Two men walking into the bus station

'Ma brother's wee boy is a right character. That wean comes oot wi' whoppers aw the time. His parents should've called him Boris.'

At the change machine outside the toilets in Buchanan Bus Station

'Thirty pence tae have a pee! Ridiculous. I'd rather wet masel'.'

Queue for coach at stance 48

Woman says, 'Let me through. Ah'm on this bus.'

Man says, 'An' whit dae ye think the rest o' us are staunin' here fur, eh? The good o' oor health? Get yer erse tae where it belongs. At the back.'

Queen Street Railway Station

Two middle-aged ladies talking at West George Street entrance

'Anyway, if ye ask me aboot "you know who", Ah think she is crazy aboot the opposite sex. Ah shouldn't really say this, but if you're ever lookin' fur her, you'll find her under the nearest man.'

Man and woman chatting at Dundas Street entrance

'Anyways, how come you're so smart, eh?'

'Och, just things Ah learned at ma mother's knee an' other low joints!'

Two ladies talking outside Lost Property

'See when oor Sheila leans tae wan side, she usually lets aff a silent wan.'

Man apparently talking about his partner

'The tidiest and most houseproud wumman Ah ever met. Dae ye know, Ah've goat tae take ma shoes aff an' blow ma nose afore she'll let me in.'

Younger women talking about a friend

'Says she lives a champagne and caviar lifestyle.'

'Mair like Irn-Bru an' pizza if ye ask me!'

Woman talking to another outside downstairs toilets

'See men. They never grow up. We were merrit when we wur 17 an' Ah virtually had tae potty train him.'

Two women having a blether

'See ma sister, she'd believe anything. Bought some perfume at the Barras because the guy said it would have Brad Pitt chappin' at her door.'

Two older men standing chatting at destination board

'How's it goin', then?'

'Aw, don't start me. Let me tell ye there's nae fool like an old fool.'

'Aye. Unfortunately ye cannae beat experience is whit Ah say.'

Man just off a train exuberantly greeting a woman at the barrier

'Here Ah am, pet! You called me. Jist keep rubbing. Noo whit's yer other two wishes?'

George Square

Man, probably the father, to hard-pressed young wife

'That wean's doin' ma heid in. Fur goodnesssake gie him milk or gie his pram a wee shoogle.'

Two ladies standing together

'See her, she's mair blonde than the dye in her hair. Everybody knows aboot her. Me, the polis, Santa Claus an' the bogey man up oor stairs.'

Farewell from woman at bus stop

'Right, that's me away. Ah'm late fur this dysfunctional family o' mine.'

Two women

'Her! She's the only wan Ah know that immediately goes intae the toilets in Morrisons afore she goes roon the shop fur her messages. Likes tae keep hersel tidy fur the CCTV, she says.'

Couple talking to Ukrainian refugees in centre of George Square

'Diz ony o' youse yins talk Scottish?'

Observation by a passer-by

'See all they pigeons. Ah bet you some of them are homing racing pigeons that thought they would just have a well-earned retirement in George Square.'

Two men talking

'Ah've got tae keep apologising fur him. He's far too rude. Even said to his brither recently that if he wanted tae hear fae an arsehole he'd fart.'

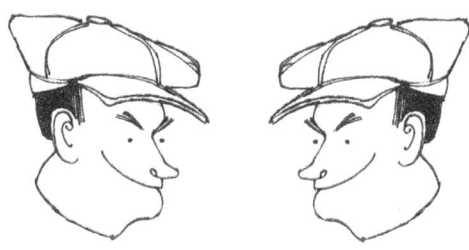

Two ladies watching a group of boys who are all singing, 'Here we go! Here we go! Here we go!'

'Wonder where that lot are goin' to, eh?'

From a group of young men

'Aw ma passwords are teachers Ah didnae like at the school.'

'You must have plenty of passwords!'

Two young women chatting

'Ah wisnae goin' tae their rotten auld wedding even if they asked me. Then they didnae ask me an' Ah wis fair bealin'!'

Man crossing George Square is approached by seedy looking individual

'Any change, mate?'

'Listen, why don't you just sell *The Big Issue* on Argyle Street if you need money?'

'Naw. Ye meet a better class o' people here.'

Two women having serious chat, one lady apparently talking about getting herself out of bad moods

'Whit Ah always say is, don't be bad moody, just shake yer booty!'

Woman bending down to clap a small dog looks up at the owner

'How old?'

'Well, if you're askin', Ah'm 51 and Stella is ten months.'

Man greeting woman walking across George Square

'An' Ah've jist goat tae ask ye, Isabel. Whit's this thing attached tae yer handbag?'

'Sure, that's ma lucky rabbit's foot.'

'Didnae help the rabbit o'er much, did it? Ye should try lucky white heather.'

Ladies sitting on a bench having a chinwag

'Him! He never maks the same mistake twice. Five or six times is mair like it.'

Two women blethering

'Thick! His bahookie is bigger than his brain is whit ma mither actually said afore we goat merrit.'

Young girls chatting

'She's apparently got tattoos everywhere. Can you imagine letting a man tattoo you on your "you know where"?'

'Depends if he wis good looking.'

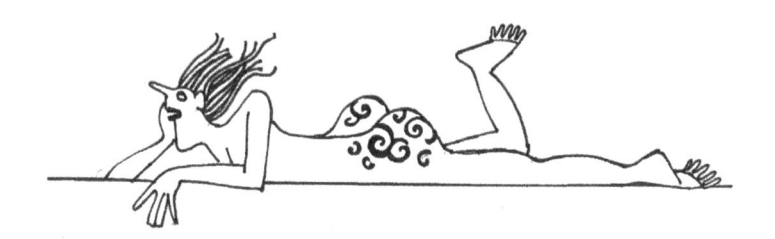

Buchanan Street

Girls chatting and giggling

'See trying tae find an attractive man in Glesca, it's like trying to find a fart in a swimming pool.'

Woman explaining her ironing technique to a friend

'Ur you kiddin'? Ah'm lazy. Ah dae aw ma ironing in ma dryer. Saves ye time, see?'

Two slightly overweight fellows walking slowly down Buchanan Street

'Ah'm goin' tae nae gym. Ah get enough exercise jist pushin' ma luck.'

Young woman passing beggar

'Change, musses?'

'Good idea. Can you change a tenner for me?'

'Sorry, hen. Cannae help. Ah'm skint.'

'That's a pity,' she says, walking straight on.

Stranger asking someone for directions to the Central Station

'Jist go doon two streets an' turn west.'

'Which way is west?'

Two men looking up at statue

'See that Donald Dewar statue. See his hauns are roon his back. He looks like a defender at a corner kick that disnae want tae gie away a penalty.'

Two ladies chatting

'I see on the internet that our local undertakers have been taken over by the Co-operative Funeral Service.'

'Probably couldnae compete wi' the stiff competition.'

Two women standing chatting

'The poor auld soul next door tae us is noo deaf in wan eye.'

Two young women

'Six weeks efter they two nights wi' Brian, Ah took wan o' they pregnancy tests.'

'And are ye preggars?'

'Naw, jist a bit overweight, Ah think.'

Women discussing health

'His breathing is awfa poor. Doesn't help himself. He's a bit o' a chain smoker.'

'Aye. That wid be the link.'

Two passing women

'Ah'm fair scunnered the day. Ah'm gonnae have tae have a wee word wi' masel when Ah get hame.'

Couple of men talking football

'Ah don't know why they signed him. He couldnae hit a coo on the backside wi' an electric banjo.'

From a group of younger women

'She says when she sees her ex her lips are on fire.'

'That wumman needs tae drink mair water!'

Embarrassed older man being helped to his feet by a passing stranger

'Naw, Ah didnae fa' doon. Ah jist thought the pavement needed a wee hug! Anyway, Ah'm thinking o' goin' oan *Strictly Come Dancing*.'

Ladies walking up the street

'Ma partner says that if they're no' talkin' aboot ye, then yer no' interesting.'

'Aye, an' there's plenty tae talk aboot wi' him.'

'Listen to who's talking! Your man's got a mooth oan him like the Clyde Tunnel.'

Young ladies chatting

'I'd really like to become politically active.'

'In which party?'

'Any party that'll have me.'

Couple of mates chatting

'If you personally cannae laugh at yersel then Ah could help you oot if ye like.'

Woman with a pizza box in her hand shouts

'Anybuddy want a slice? Ah'm no' as hungry as Ah though Ah wis.'

From a passing woman: 'Gie it tae the guy beggin' doon the street. His dug wull eat it.'

Two ladies discussing men

'Ah can aye tell when he wants sex. You know, he gie's me that special look.'

'Ah wish sometimes ma man would gie me that look.'

Two friends meeting

'How's married life treating you, then?'

'We're no' speaking today. Don't ask me. Och no, I'll tell you. He's getting more like his mother every day.'

Two men walking and talking

'Inflation just means we will all have to work harder.'

'Aye, Ah'll probably need tae work harder at not gettin' a job.'

Two men chatting

'The trouble is when ye meet him ye cannae get away fae him. There definitely must be a donkey somewhere in Glesca wi' its back legs missing.'

Beggar sitting shouting at passing woman

'Get a bigger handbag, hen. Then ye could pit mair money in it tae gie tae scum like me.'

Two men meet

'Oh, it's you, Brian.'

'Aye, it's me. Ah'll say this, at least ye don't need tae go tae Specsavers.'

Men sorting out the world's problems

'See seagulls. Very aggressive birds. Ah wid cull them. Mind you, Ah've goat an aggressive bird Ah live with.'

Overheard from a loud bunch of passing football supporters

'You should understand, mate, if Ah agreed wi' ye aw oor supporters wid be wrang, tae!'

Guy with guitar and amplifier stops singing to ask for requests

Man shouts, 'Aye. Piss aff roon the corner an' play in Gordon Street.'

Two ladies chatting

'Unfortunately, I have an anxiety disorder now, Jenny, an' Ah've a sore big toe tae.'

Two older ladies talking

'I was looking online at one of these cremation only companies. Makes sense. Would save a lot of hassle.'

'No way! My family have given me a lot of hassle so I want the full works.'

Two men apparently talking about a forthcoming darts match

'Easy peasy, bumbaleezi. That'll be a right skoosh. Sure, Ah'm an expert at hitting the bull.'

'Aye, the pub, ye mean.'

Tourist holding umbrella

'Is it always raining so hard in Glasgow?'

'No, no, no. It's just a very high tide today.'

Men chatting

'He's stopped using hair shampoo noo that he's as bald as a billiard ball. Just uses a wee drap o' Fairy.'

Two girls

'This guy wis layin' it oan thick that Byres Road wisnae aw that hot. She got angry an' said he obviously had nae taste. Anyway, the end o' their argy-bargy wis that they are going on a date tae a restaurant in Byres Road. Wid make ye laugh.'

Couple of men putting the world to rights

'I read on the internet that I will be the last person to die in my lifetime.'

'Wow. That's profound. Would put you off dying.'

Two women suddenly meeting

'Oh! Zippidee-doo-dah, it's yersel, Frances!'

Two older ladies chatting about the weather

'Ah love when it's warm, but Ah hate humidity.'

'Well, we're lucky, ye don't really get much humility in Glesca.'

Two women talking

'Ye see, ma upbringing wis jist an emotional mess. An' so's ma marriage, noo.'

'Oh, right.'

Cheeky passer-by to woman sorting her hair while using a window to catch her reflection

'Aye, yer right, hen. Ye need tae get yersel a herrcut.'

Two couples chatting. One man obviously a linguist

'Ah husnae problemos wi' ma communicatio in Spainio.'

Two women

'Acts like she's Cinderella, a goody-two-shoes type. Probably never hame afore midnight.'

Man meeting friend

'Jimmy, ye look harassed.'

'Listen. Ah'm jist tryin' tae find ma tail so Ah can catch it.'

Woman apparently complaining to a male friend that she has difficulty losing weight

'Ah wish Ah wis mair athletic.'

'Well, if you ask me yer aye awfa good at jumpin' tae conclusions.'

Woman to man

'Naw, Ah cannae walk that far. Ma legs are older than yours.'

'Jist yer legs?'

Two girls standing together, one of them on her mobile

'Naw, Paul. Listen. Ah told ye Ah'm at the gym.'

Other girl looks at her and in a softer voice says, 'Ya lying bitch!'

Two women

'He's got dreadful bad breath! Believe me, you couldnae tell a yawn fae a fart.'

Man and woman talking

'Apparently somebody at Glasgow Airport told her she looks like Meghan Markle. Well, Ah cannae see any prince flying in tae take her tae America, can you?'

Two ladies walking

'Ah wis oot fur a walk wi' the dog roon the Necropolis on Sunday. You should see they monuments. You know, some o' they rich folks live in luxury.'

Couple of guys passing

'Ma wife's cousin is the laziest man I've ever heard of. Hasnae worked fur years an' years. The only job he'd ever apply for wid be as a thumb-twiddler wi' the Council.'

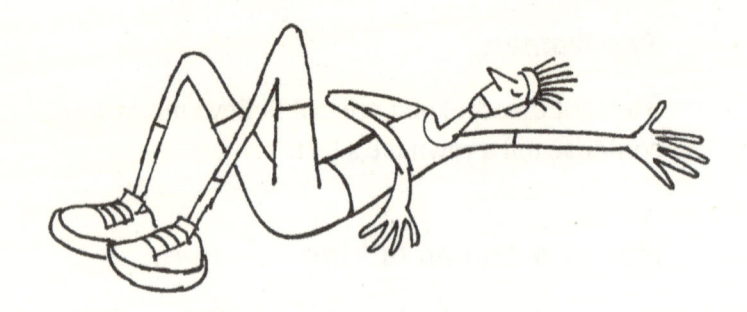

From a group of men talking

'Ah'm a bit old fur joggin'. Anyways, have ye ever seen a jogger smiling? And it's nae good fur yer knees. An' another thing. If we ever have a famine, aw they thin joggers will die first.'

Two women

'See since ma first lot o' vaccine, Ah've been right intae eatin' egg an' chips. Never liked eggs afore.'

Two women talking

'Says he would like tae be oan *Mastermind* an' he didnae even remember ma birthday. Ah gave him hell.'

Observation by man to another

'Naw, naw. Ah don't believe in Santa Claus, ghosts or even weather forecasts. In fact, they're the worst.'

Couple of older men

'People think that Marian vapes a lot but it's just her inhaler for asthma.'

Two ladies discussing an impending wedding.

'She's no chicken tae be gettin' merrit at her age.'

'Ye can say that again. But knowing her, Ah bet he'll be henpecked.'

Two young women

'Ah wis actually thinkin' o' maybe havin' a baby.'

'Thinkin' isnae goin' tae dae it. It needs something mair than that, you know.'

Ladies chatting

'Went tae Nice fur a couple o' days an' apparently it wis during the film festival there. Noo he walks aboot Glesca like he's a celebrity. Wull probably be starring at the Hydro soon!'

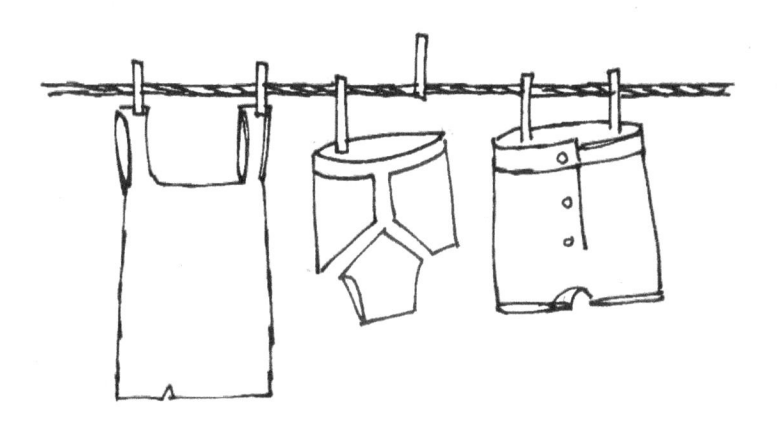

Couple arguing

'Listen you! When we goat merrit, aw you had wis two pairs o' underpants an' a vest. If ye don't behave yersel, ye can go and take yer underpants and yer vest wi' ye.'

'Keep yer voice down. Yer gie'n me a big riddie.'

Men apparently talking about an acquaintance

'Watch him carefully. A right bamboozier if ever there was one.'

'Bamboozier?'

'Aye, ye know, an aggressive drunk.'

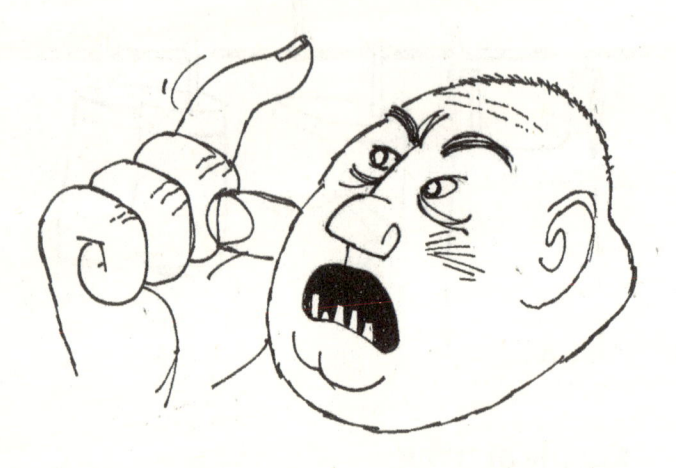

Women discussing health

'She's gone vegan. Crazy! Lives jist next tae a kebab shop.'

Throwaway comment from a group of young women

'Our auld nan just leaves her Christmas lights up all year. Doesnae turn them on in the summer, though. Says it saves her electricity bill.'

Women talking

'Ma cousin in London has asked me tae get him tickets fur the Edinburgh Mahogany Street Party this New Year.'

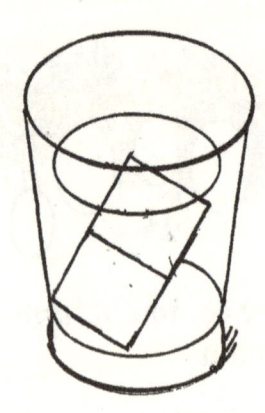

Couple of ladies chatting

'Noo Ah'm at an age when the only frozen dessert ma doctor recommends is an ice cube in ma G and T.'

Women discussing the youth of today

'It's awright fur the youth o' today. Ah've had ma youth, but the youth o' today have mair freedoms.'

'The question is, tae dae whit?'

'Unfortunately, anything they like, it would appear.'

Couple of guys

'If ever there wis a smart-ass, it's him. Wan o' these days he's goin' tae meet himsel comin' back.'

Two couples chatting

'Ah don't know how she ended up wi' him. Probably booze an' poor judgement.'

Older women on the weather

'See during that hot spell, Ah think it wis awfa funny seein' aw they auld men in their shorts wi' wee white, skinny legs like celery sticks.'

Two young women

'He wis cheatin' oan her.'

'Aye, but did you naw know she wis cheatin' oan him, tae?'

Sauchiehall Street

Two younger girls

'Ma mither keeps askin' who the faither is. Really, it's nane o' her business. Anyways, Ah'm pretty sure it's either Frank or that Sean.'

Two men chatting away

'Ah goat cheap flights tae Ibiza fur the five o' us. Cheap ma erse! By the time Ah paid fur speedy boardin', legroom an' luggage, Ah nearly had tae extend ma mortgage.'

Two older men

'Ah missed Jack's funeral. Got the wrong day in ma head. Anyway, he'll never know, will he?'

Group of well-dressed ladies standing gossiping

'His dial looks like a well-skelped arse.'

The other ladies look askance at each other at this language.

Two younger men

'She keeps failing her driving tests. Ah told her the only way tae pass wis tae wear wan o' her wee miniskirts next time.'

Two men laughing

'A wis readin' that they MSPs jist agreed a rise in their wages and allowances. Just goes tae show they're no' as daft as we thought.'

Two women suddenly meet

'Nice tae see you again but Ah need tae skedaddle aff! Ta-ta-the-noo.'

A complaining woman

'John's a right lazy lump. He jist sits in front of the telly wi' his thumb in his bum an' his mind in neutral!'

Older woman shouting to her male companion

'Haud ma teeth till Ah tie ma lace!'

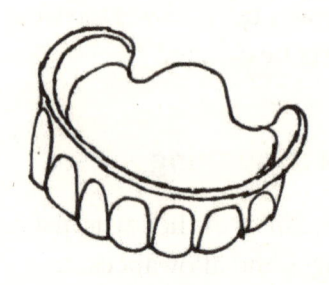

Two women standing listening to busker playing a trumpet

'Och Ah'm away hame tae ma man. He's another wan who's always blowing his ain trumpet.'

Two men chatting

'Let me tell you, if it wisnae fur Google half the population o' Scotland wid be totally ignorant.'

Two women

'He's absolutely useless. Didn't even wash the lavvy pot properly this morning.'

From a group of four women

'I got fed up with oor wee Sammy sitting playing games on his phone. So Ah hid it. Gave it tae him back after a couple of hours as he wis driving me mad.'

Couple of men

'Him! Holds onto everything for himself. Would give you hee-haw. A right constipated clunker if ever there was one.'

Group of women

'Must be wan of the unluckiest men in Glasgow. Wis at the Royal fur outpatient treatment fur ulcers on his leg. Came oot the front door, fell doon and broke his other leg. At least he wis in the right place tae get it fixed and have a stookie pit oan.'

Two women

'And as fur her. Never smells right, you know. She's as fresh as a pub carpet.'

Two women moaning about cost of living

'See ma purse. It's like an onion. Every time Ah open it, it makes me cry.'

Two young women

'See if Ah give ma five-year-old chips, he goes at them like a frog swallowing midges.'

Two guys chatting

'See efter watchin' that movie, Ah'm full o' popcorn an' revenge.'

Women chatting

'She's aff the wall. In fact, aff her heid. Imagine that as yer next-door neighbour.'

Two women meeting

'Listen, Eleanor, ye widnae believe it, but Ah've just bought a pair o' boots an' Ah only came oot the hoose this morning tae go and buy totty scones.'

Man carrying door

Passer-by shouts, 'Did ye lose yer keys, pal?'

Two men chatting

'An' oor poor auld paw is getting mair wobbly an' clappit oot by the day. Ah doot another clean shirt wull dae him.'

HIRPLE

Men discussing money

'Apparently shoplifting is on the increase due to cost-of-living problems. But when you get to supermarket check-outs, there are umpteen o' these self-service machines. So really, they're asking for it! Sure they is?'

Two men chatting

'Ah've known her fur years. She's goat a smile oan her like a Cooncil rent collector.'

Two ladies

'My husband says to me to always give a hundred per cent in whatever you do. So, I just said to him why don't ye go an' gie blood, ya big dope.'

Two ladies

'Oor next-door neighbour has been waiting on a new hip for over two years.'

'An' Ah've been waiting on a new man for mair years than that.

Two men

'Forty-five years of marital disharmony, but let me tell you, they jist love aw their arguments. That's whit keeps them thegither.'

Sisters talking

'It's amazing. Ah don't feel Ah'm old, but when oor granny wis ma age she had been deid fur at least seven years.'

Two women

'Thon wee wean o' hers is a caution. In fact, he's a right belter.'

Young ladies

'How's that new guy you've been going out with?'

'Nearly adequate.'

Two men chatting

'Ah wis awfa happy tae hear oor local crematorium noo has baith cremators back up an' workin'.'

'Oh, my. You're easily pleased!'

Ladies blethering

'She is really laid-back. Takes life with a pinch of salt, she says.'

'A pinch? Aye, that'll be right. Ah've seen her knockin' back plenty o' margaritas.'

Two older men

'Told me he wis in a wee pickle an' then asked fur a loan o' two hunner pounds. "That's no' a wee pickle," says I.'

Group of boys standing outside a shop

Suddenly one says, 'Errapolis cummin'!'

'Jist stay cool. We're daein' nothing wrang. Wull dae wrang later.'

Men talking about an acquaintance

'Yon's an odd kind o' fellow. He asks you a question and then answers it himself.'

'Anyway, it saves you thinkin' aboot it, eh?'

Two young women

'See ma family, we're aw different. Aw ma brithers and sisters have nothing in common really. The only thing that runs in oor family is noses and diarrhoea.'

Two women on the youth of today

'The kids o' today know everythin' aboot sex. Sex education in schools is a waste o' time. Like givin' a goldfish a bath. Oor mithers wid die wi' their legs up.'

Two women

'Och, ye know fine who Ah'm talkin' aboot. It's hingmy that's merrit tae wee shooies' brither.'

Couple of older men

'Talk, talk, talk! She's like a dug yapping at a postman.'

Two women gossiping

'Posh! Wan o' her neighbours told me she has tae put oan her earrings tae go an' collect deliveries fae the Amazon driver.'

Two women

'See ma Sheila, she shaves aw her legs and then moans because she didnae need tae as she jist wears jeans wi' only wee bits ripped aff.'

Young guy begging

'Ah've maxed oot my credit card again. Any chance o' a quid?'

Two women meeting and greeting two others

'Oh, hello there. Long time no see. How are you both getting on?'

'Fine. How about you?'

'Fine.'

All the ladies eventually move on. One set of women look at each another.

'You'll need tae remind me. Who were these two?'

Two ladies apparently pulling an acquaintance to bits

'Somebody told me thingummyjig went tae a slimming club an' got stuck in their door. Ye've goat tae laugh. An' Ah've never seen such skinny legs. Reminds me o' wishbones at Christmas.'

Two ladies

'Tell that wee toerag nuthin'. A right wee clype if ever there wis wan.'

Two men

'Thinks he's superior. Ye know, born wi' a silver spoon up his jacksie.'

Men chatting

'I'll say this for him. Doesn't have a care in the world. And he could paper his wall with all the parking tickets he's had. Jist cracks me up, so he does.'

Two ladies talking

'Maist days he's like an alligator fae Govan.'

'Ah don't think ye get alligators in Govan.'

'Aye, whitever. Ye know whit Ah mean.'

Two women

'That wan reckons he'll go far in this life. That's a laugh for a start. He's hardly ever been oot o' Glasgow.'

Two young ladies talking

'He said he likes women with good posture. Ah've a hunch he meant me. Ha ha.'

Couple apparently discussing his visits to the pub

'Aye, an' if ye go don't let the door hit yer erse on the way.'

Two women

'She's put on a fair bit o' weight. Must be some sight in the scuddy.'

Two women chatting

'You couldnae say anything nice aboot her, no' really. Not Brain o' Britain and extremely plain. Her mother probably got an apology letter fae Durex.'

Two guys watching a busker vigorously walloping a drum

'Great tune that. Ye canny beat it.'

Argyle Street

Two men

'Don't tell me ye've broken yer arm?'

'Aye. Missed a step an' fell arse over tit.'

Two pensioners standing chatting

'She's been at the doctor for years and years. Always doon at their Health Centre. Says she needs tae find hersel. Well, Ah widnae want tae find her. Aye goat something like tennis elbow or sore knees or something. Nae wunner other normal folks cannae get an appointment wi' a doctor.'

Two men meeting

'Ur ye awright, big man? For goodness' sake did somebuddy cut yer hair wi' a knife an' fork? Jist tell me their name an' Ah'll get them fur ye!'

Two women

'Whit he says wid blow yer socks aff. An' efter livin' wi' him fur over 30 years Ah can tell ye he has dreadful smelly feet.'

Two women

'Him! He's no' a kick in the pants aff stupidity.'

Couple of women

'Noo he says he's a problem wi' his gizzards, whitever they may be.'

Man and woman chatting

'Our stupid neighbours have got themselves a new dog. Seems tae growl aw the time.'

'Probably barking mad.'

'Oh, very droll.'

Two women

'I suspect he has a very low IQ. Probably the thickest man this side o' the Mississippi.'

'Oh. Why the Mississippi?'

'Cause he probably couldnae even spell it.'

Two women talking

'See ma Charles this morning, Ah could have killed him. The idiot just sits there in his favourite chair saying, "Ah don't know whit tae dae wi' masel." So Ah jist told him whit he should do wi' himsel!'

Two women

'He's noo on 20 milligrams every day.'

'Och, ma brither was oan 200 milligrams a day.'

'No way! If he took that amount he'd be deid.'

'Aye. He's deid.'

Two men

'Where ur ye goin' fur yer holidays this year?'

'Uch. Hamildaeme.'

'Well, at least ye'll no need a visa.'

Two groups of women meet and talk

'Ye should hear her speak noo. We wis brought up thegether an' noo she talks pan loaf.'

Two men apparently talking about slow service in a café

'Nice looking lass, but isnae over bright, ye know. Wid need a hunner-watt bulb an' a battery up her arse tae function properly.'

Two couples chatting

'We jist came back fae Lanzarote yesterday. Oor pilot came on the blower an' said we could expect a few bumps an' moderate turbulence. Let me tell you Ah huvnae been juggled up an' doon like that since Ah sat oan ma mammy's knee.'

Two older ladies

'She jist loves goin' doon tae Millport fur the day. She's there that much she's probably liable fur Council tax.'

Two elderly men

'Ah wis in the butcher's section in oor supermarket. See the price o' meat. Let me tell you, Shylock couldnae afford a pound o' flesh in there.'

Two men

'Half o' whit they politicians say is mince an' the other half is burnt toast. Nothin' but a bunch o' doolies.'

Man making observation about something

'In the name o' ma mammy, daddy and oor lodger's wee dug, whit ur they playin' at? Eh?'

Two ladies

'How is Betty this weather?'

'Oh, wonder woman? Aye, everybody keeps wondering whit she's up tae.'

Observation from woman as two boys pass

'That wee fellow should wear better earphones. Dreadful taste in music. Silly boy!'

Two young guys

'Huh! Rugby is nuffin' but pushin', shovin' an' kickin' the other team. Footie is mair skillful an' gentle.'

'Gentle! Ye've goat tae be at the kiddin'!'

Two men

'Where have you been, Michael?'

'There an' back.'

'Glad ye came back!'

Two women

'They two sisters you know are weird. They knock aboot wi' the same man. Ah wunner how that works?'

'Nae idea. Anyway, it's goat the square root o' tuppence tae dae wi' me.'

Man talking to friend while waiting for wife outside shop

'Ma wife gets whit she calls winter blues. So, she bought a sunlamp. Now says it's been nae good. Jist puts up the electricity bill.'

Two women

'Him! Thon's a dirty bit o' yellow snow!'

Two women

'Forgets everything. Aw his memories are in his bum.'

'Whit dae ye mean?'

'Behind him.'

Two older women

'Did you see that programme last night aboot reincarnation? Frightening. Imagine havin' tae go through aw this again wi' men, babies an' things.'

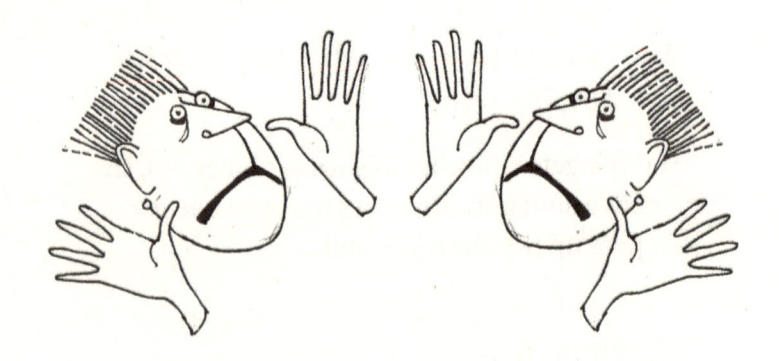

Two women

'You know Ah'm fed up listening tae him. Been on the *Waverley* twice in the last month and now thinks he's Barnacle Bill.'

Two men

'He's let himsel go something terrible. Looks like a half-pun o' mince hingin' aff a hook.'

Two women

'Talk aboot a lack o' hygiene. She's goat a breath on her like a deid budgie.'

Two Couples

'And see him, he got two fillings, and tae hear him moanin' ye wid think he'd had a heart transplant.'

Two men

'Actually, she thinks she's a bit o' hot stuff.'

'Whit! She's 70 if she is a day. Doesnae even walk right. Jist waddles.'

Two young girls

'How did your blind date go?'

'A waste o' lipstick, makeup and time, if you ask me. An' the eejit wants tae see me again. Nae chance!'

Two young ladies

'We had just got into the restaurant when he put his hand in his pocket for a paper tissue and out fell a condom. At that time Ah couldnae make up ma mind if it wis an accident or a wee hint. Anyways, by the end of the night it was well used.'

Two young women

'See when Ah have ma period, Ah jist go tae McDonalds and gie masel a wee treat.'

Two women

'Listen tae me, Helen. Ah don't have time fur this nonsense. He's a right heidbanger and that's aw there is tae it.'

Two men

'See they energy bills. Heavens, Ah can remember when gas only went up when ye put a match tae it. An' electricity can be shockin', tae.'

'Aye, if ye stick yer finger in the socket.'

Two women talking

'So where's yer better half the day?'

'Oh, he's strippin' aff auld paint fae a table. Says he wants tae find out the unvarnished truth. A right comedian that one.'

Two men

'He's goat a smart mooth but husnae a smart brain.'

Two women

'With his wife's passing, that's him on his own now. The poor man will starve. Couldnae even fry Rice Crispies.'

Two men

'It's baltic the day, intit? Colder than a brickie's bum for sure.'

Couples talking. Woman says

'We've been married for over 30 years and still have a close relationship.'

Husband replies, 'Close relationship? Whit relationship ur ye talking about?'

'Now, Walter, don't let me down.'

Two women

'I am gluten intolerant and have been for a while.'

'Are you sure it's not just intolerant?'

Two women

'Ah wis fat as a baby, Ah'm still fat and Ah'll be fat when Ah'm in ma box.'

Two women

'She says he's workin' overtime every night. Doesnae come hame till efter midnight.'

'Sounds a bit skew-whiff, if ye ask me.'

Two men

'Huv ye seen wee Davie of late? Awfa thin. Barely eight stones wringin' wet.'

Two women

'That wan is never oot o' aw they city centre clubs an' pubs. Ah bet ye that wee boy o' hers wis conceived oan a pool table!'

'Well, she's certainly snookered, noo.'

Woman continually being pestered by a small boy who apparently wants a new toy

'Lester, how many times have I got tae tell you. No. Spelled N.O.! My indecision is absolutely final. Ah'll be havin' a wee hissy in a minute.'

Man talking to woman

'Ah heard oor neighbour's boy wis caught shopliftin' again. They should call him Batman. You know, cannae go oot without Robin.'

Two women

'She's forever at the doctor getting new medicine. Has goat mair pills in her than Boots the Chemist.'

Two older ladies

'Ma sister who is now in her 70s wis complaining she finds it difficult keepin' up wi' technology. Says the problem is this is the first time she's been old!'

Woman discussing health issues with husband

'As you know, Ah always go fur high fibre foods. Keeps me regular.'

'Ye can say that again, pet. Sure, every time Ah need the lavvy, you're in it!'

Two women

'An' then the doctor sounded me.'

'Yer chest?'

'Well, it widnae be ma heid, wid it?'

Group of men

'He's not got a great deal of confidence. Needs tae mature. You know the type. Will never have a shiver running up his back cause that wan is spineless.'

Two young women

'She kids oan she's a shrinkin' violet but she's mair like a dangerous dandelion.'

Two men

'Ah told ye that Scottish Government wur a bunch o' animals. Aye looking fur scapegoats, ma man says.'

Two women

'He switches me right aff!'

'Listen. He switches everybuddy right aff!'

Two women

'Noo he says he wants an electric car. You've goat tae laugh. We're still oan a pre-payment meter.'

Two women

'Her husband has been a postman for over 20 years. Probably keeps him fit.'

'Well, wi' the price o' stamps nooadays Ah hope he noo walks a bit faster.'

Two older women

'Weight is really sneaky. Ah keep tryin' tae lose it but the rascal always finds me.'

Woman to teenage boy, apparently her son

'So, whit did yer faither ask ye tae get him fae Tesco?'

'That fat bird on the faraway checkout!'

'Dirty auld rascal.'

Man shouting to another

'Hey, big man! Ur ye okay? Yer wanderin' aboot like a fart in a trance.'

Two women

'Ma brother-in-law thinks he's God's gift tae women. Thinks he's film star material. Actually, he's nothing but a big, lanky, loose-limbed wally.'

Two women

'Ah've been tellin' him to tidy his room for ages noo. He's 15. Jist ignores me an' gives me the rubber ear.'

'Ah wid try givin' him a sore ear.'

Two young women

'They say the planet is getting hotter and hotter, unlike ma Iain – he is getting colder and mair stiff.'

'Try antifreeze an' WD40.'

Two women

'Me an' Peter watched oor wedding video last night. The wedding was nearly 30 years ago and ten o' the guests have died and two couples have divorced.'

'At least you two are still together.'

'Aye. Just!'

Two women

'There's only 16 months between ma sister an' masel. But Ah can always remember fighting wi' her tae who wis got in the big pram an' who wis in the wee wan.'

Two women

'Unfortunately, she is useless in company. Jist stands there like a right wally.'

'Yer right. She's goat the split personality o' a cake whisk an' a microwave.'

Two women

'I am never going with him to another football match. See all this hollering, chanting and singing. They all act like chimpanzees on happy pills.'

Two women

'Ma mother always said life is like the hokey kokey an' it's never too late tae turn yersel around.'

Two women chatting

'Him! Talks oot the side o' his mooth and other bits o' him, tae.'

Glasgow Subway

Queue on platform

'See that woman wi' the yellow raincoat o'er there. Let me tell you she wid gie onybuddy a double dose o' the black boak.'

Crowd on escalator

'He's an absolute wee toerag. Ah even heard his ain mither calling him a son o' a bitch.'

Two women

'Huv ye seen her latest hairstyle? By the looks o' it, Ah think she must use a lavvy brush.'

Ladies having loud discussion

'Ah think the government should stop aw they adverts in the middle o' TV programmes. Fair spoils the hale thing if you ask me.'

Man talking to women

'He has given up rugby for a few weeks following his percussion.'

Woman making an observation

'Whit Ah say is that at least if ye fa' asleep on the underground, aw ye dae is go roon an' roon.'

Two couples talking

'Ah'm worried aboot that wan. Clueless an' glaikit, so she is.'

Two men talking football

'He's pigeon-toed. An' wi' legs that should have a message tied tae them.'

Two women

'Fairly keeps you awake wi' the carriages rattlin' intae tunnels at a hunner miles an hour, sure it does?'

Two men

'He is very sensitive. Bruises awfa easily.'

'And he's a referee?'

Two young women

'The paur soul is jist no' comfortable in his own skin.'

'Aye, well, he's no' gettin' intae mine.'

Two women

'Ah don't know how she sticks wi' him. She should give him the old heave-ho.'

Central Station Concourse

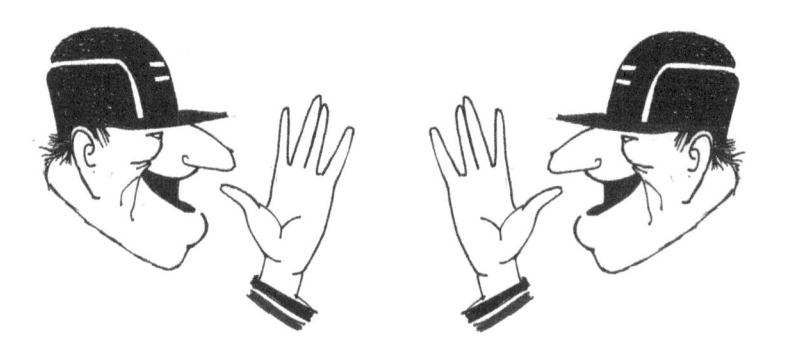

Railway official at platform six

'Good news and bad news, folks. The good news is that your train will be coming into this platform. The bad news is it's running about an hour late.'

Two older men at destination board

'Ah've been tryin' tae understaun' ma wife's moods fur over 40 years, and Ah'm still totally confused.'

Two women

'At least wi' a nose like hers it wid save ye buying a tin opener.'

Two women

'See ma auntie and uncle, they've been merrit fur nearly 50 years an' they still bicker aw the time. Ye see, wan's Celtic an' the ither is Rangers.'

Two women looking up at destination board

'Ah heard her say in the hairdressers she was approaching 39. Ah've heard her say that fur years noo. Everybuddy is frightened tae ask, "Aye, but fae which direction?"'

Two men

'Ah wid say it's squeaky bum time fur the whole team, no' just the manager.'

Two men in seating area

'There wis a documentary oan the other night and someone said that we are all alone in the universe. Ah think that's a pity. It wid be great fun tae go to another planet that has a Glesca oan it. Might even have better weather. Save ye goin' abroad.'

Two men chatting

'The only advantage o' Covid wis that ma sister-in-law's infectious laugh was covered up by a mask.'

Woman meeting friend outside WH Smith

'Oh, hello, Jean. Sorry Ah'm a wee bit late. We aw had curry last night an' Ah couldnae stop sittin' oan the lavvy-pan this morning.'

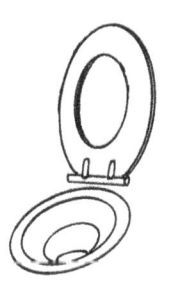

Two couples chatting

'Hey, Jack. How's retirement going?'

'Smashing. Aw ma life Ah've had tae knock ma pan in, so this is magic.'

And his wife said, 'An' noo Ah've goat tae knock ma pan in lookin' after him an' the hoose.'

Two women

'Ma sister's the same. Doesnae take care o' her appearance. Her hair's aye clingin' an' mingin'.'

Two women

'Ah've heard o' people being born so ugly that they skelped the mother. In his case they probably battered the doctor an' the stork, tae.'

Two women walking towards Gordon Street entrance

'Did ye see her photo on Facebook? Probably Photoshopped.'

Couple of men in seating area

'I heard he was off work with a bad chest complaint.'

'Well, my question is simple. Is he still breathing?'

'Yea.'

'Good, cause we're aw going oot oan Saturday.'

Two women

'An' see that new hairstyle o' hers, looks like sticky candyfloss oot fur a walk in the rain.'

Two younger men

'Absolutely no way. Yer totally wrong. Yer bum wid be oot the windae if it wisnae sae cauld.'

Two women

'It's funny. Ah'm called Margaret and ma sister is Agnes. Really quite ordinary names. But oor two brothers are called Duggie an' Shuggie.'

'How is that funny?'

Two men

'Wee Richard keeps asking where babies come from. Ma wife told him that the stork brings babies, but he didnae like that answer. So Ah told him ye order them on Amazon and he seems to have accepted that.'

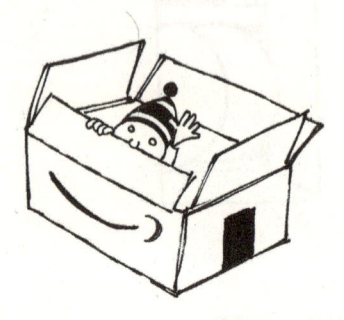

Two women

'He might be a toaty wee man, but he's really a cheeky wee nyaff, so he is.'

Two women

'Ah could see he wis gettin' angry so Ah jist said tae him, "don't you dare spit yer dummy oot at me!"'

Two women meeting at flower shop

'Hello, Jean. My, yer fair pittin' the beef oan.'

'Naw Ah'm naw. It's this new coat o' mine. Look who is talking.'

Two men

'Whit dae ye mean Ah'm too old tae dae that sort of thing? Ah'm only just 70. That's the new middle age, ye know.'

'Aye. Whitever ye say yersel, grandpa.'

Two couples chatting

'He says he is a bit loose the day, so Ah jist told him tae go an' stick a cork or two in it.'

A group of women

'Where's yer mither-in-law got tae noo?

'She's nipped intae the ladies. Always running tae the loo, so she is. If her name wis Winnie she'd be called Winnie the Pooh!'

Two men

'His patter is like watter. Rehearsed patter, if you ask me.'

Two women in patisserie

'See thingamajig, he wears shorts right through the winter.'

'Is he a health freak?'

'Naw. An attention seeker.'

Two women

'See when Ah met her, ma first impressions weren't good. And now that Ah know the woman my second impressions are even worse.'

Two women in Upper Crust Café

'Whit Ah'm worried aboot is aw they migraines crossin' the channel.'

Two men outside toilets

'Ye know, life is all about timing at oor age.'

'Aye, gettin' there on time before yer desperate an' aiming when yer peeing.'

Two older ladies

'We wur in Chicago visitin' his brither. Ah've goat tae say, Americans aw have better teeth than we dae.'

'Aye. Probably take them oot every night an' scrub them wi' Ajax.'

Two women

'She says she's 54 and still hasn't had the "change". Talk aboot lucky.'

Two women

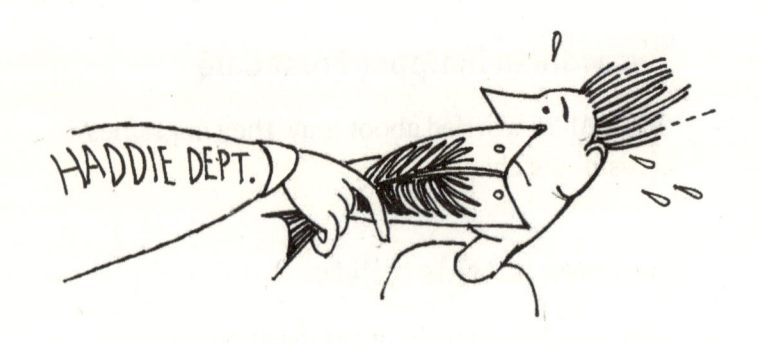

'It's ridiculous. Ma benefit payments have been cut again. Mind you, at least the money is better than a slap oan the face wi' a wet haddie. But Ah jist told them Ah need mair.'

Two men standing under clock

'He maintains he does 10,000 steps a day. More like over a month goin' tae the pub.'

Ladies chatting

'Bill says it would help if I laughed more. Says laughter is the best medicine.'

'Aye, but what if ye've goat a weak bladder, eh?'

Remark by one woman to another

'Talk aboot tight. She's the type that wid even use everybuddy else's bath water efter they've been in it.'

Two men

'He takes furever tae come oot wi' the words. A sort o' monotone whine, just like his wife.'

Observation from passing women

'That wan's aff his trolly an' it doesnae even have a pound coin in it.'

Two ladies

'We went tae a Glasgow Gin and Rum Festival a couple o' weeks back. It wis good, but we forgot we had brought the car and had tae pay a fortune in taxis.'

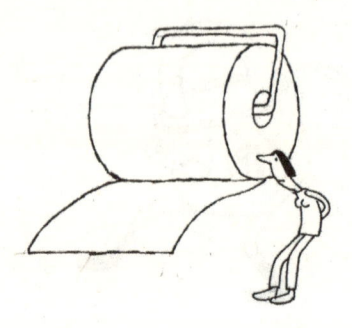

Three women in burger king

'Dae ye remember during Covid everybody was buying up toilet paper. Ah think Ah overdid it. We haven't had tae buy any noo for months.'

Two ladies

'He's on the dole noo. A shame really, as he worked his tail aff. Well, sometimes.'

Two young men

'How's yer dosh?'

'Doon tae aboot a half-pint an' a packet o' crisps.'

Two young women

'Ah met him at oor club. Noo he says Ah tick aw his boxes. He certainly doesnae even get wan tick fae me. The man's bonkers.'

Two young men at destination board

'Ah've been really careful of late. Cannae remember the last time Ah had a lot tae drink.'

'Are you at the kiddin'? You had at least six pints last night.'

'Ah cannae really remember that.'

Three men

'See oor opinions aboot things. They are jist as good as the wans they politicians have, an' they are getting paid. It's a scandal is whit Ah say.'

Two women

'Ma Auntie Jean died a couple o' days ago.'

'Oh. Sorry tae hear that.'

'Well, she wisnae really ma auntie. A sort o' kiddy-oan auntie. She just lived in the next close tae us 40 odd years ago.'

Two women

'He's a big, lazy lump. Says that hard work never hurt anybuddy but ye cannae be too careful.'

Two women

'You wouldnae believe it. Wanted tae use our holiday money tae go wi' the Tartan Army an' see Scotland playing in Germany. Ah jist said, "away an' save up fur it yersel." So noo he's no' goin'.'

Two men

'We had visitors from Germany last week. For some reason they thought Scotland was full of pirates.'

'Well, lots o' guys seem tae be wearing black beards nooadays.'

Two older men watching the antics of a group of boys

'See aw they programmes aboot wildlife in Africa. Ah'm no' interested. They should make mair programmes aboot the wildlife in Glesca. An' Ah'm no' talkin' animals.'

Two young ladies

'His mate told me he had bet him 20 quid he wid spend the night wi' me. Does he think Ah'm a racehorse? Anyway, Ah made sure he lost his money.'

Man and woman in patisserie

'Listen. What about us going to Tenerife for a week in December?'

'This is just July, John. We might be sick o' the sight o' each other come December.'

Two women in Burger King

'He's been lookin' gey peelie-wally for a while now but I didn't realise he was goin' tae go an' die oan me.'

Two women

'She needs tae look in the mirror more.'

'If you were her, would you look in the mirror more?'

Two couples

'If ye ask me, he's no' right upstairs' an' doonstairs. An' another thing, he's goat bowly legs, tae.'

Two women

'He's goin' oot wi' a refugee. Apparently in her country her family are intae oil.'

'Well, so is he. Sure, he works in a garage.'

Two men

'Listen. Let me tell you. You might get a cheeky-chappy type in somewhere like Clarkston, but no' in Castlemilk.'

Two young ladies in seating area

'What I would like is someone who is faithful, attentive and into exercising on a regular basis.'

'You need a dog.'

Two men

'Ma auld faither never ate vegetables or fruit. Loved pies and sausages, and died in his nineties. Just shows ye.'

Two women

'He's a right pain an' she's a right pain an' they've been merrit fur ages. Och, well, it's nae use spoiling two hooses as ma auld Auntie Esther used tae say.'

Upper Hope Street

Two men meeting

'Aw, it's you, Goofy. An' Ah can see ye've goat in yer new teeth!'

Young men

'Listen, Arnold. You should try to be more humorous and self-defecating. Women love that kind o' stuff.'

Two women

'She thinks they're world travellers. Pits oan airs an' graces aw because they go tae Benidorm every year.'

Two women

'One foot in the grave, ma erse. By the look on her face, that woman has had baith feet in the grave fur years but naebuddie's phoned fur the undertaker so far.'

Two men

'He's goat a funny side tae him. Likes tae be different. Probably supports Partick Thistle reserves.'

Two women

'Always up tae high doh. Always goat her knickers in a twist. An', knowin' her, she probably doesnae even wear any!'

Two women

'Words fail me when Ah think o' her. The best plan is no' tae think o' her an' they five cheeky brats o' hers.'

Group of ladies

'She's goat a great system fur gettin' younger. Takes a year aff her ain an' adds it tae her sister's age. An' the laugh is they're twins.'

Two young girls

'Are you still pregnant?'

'What a stupid question. Ma wee Lily is now three months.'

'Sorry. Ah got confused.'

Two older men

'How's your cousin Desmond?'

'Still dead. Sure, he died last year. They don't come back, you know.'

Two women

'Ah know Ah should really apologize tae her, but the way she goes on really gets half-way up ma humph.'

Women apparently discussing their partners

'Naw, wan o' they sex stimulants wid be nae good fur him. Mair like two o' sand an' wan o' cement is whit he needs.'

Group of women discussing shopping

'Some o' their claes are a bit old fashioned if you ask me. But let me tell you straight, they don't have old fashioned prices.'

Woman talking to her husband

'I am going to dye my hair again. Something perhaps a little closer to my natural colour.'

'So, you're going to dye it grey?'

'Now, that is cheeky! Very cheeky.'

Two women

'Whit a dial oan that wan, eh? If ye ask me, the coo wull want its arse back.'

Two women

'Ah'm no' saying she's past it, but probably her idea of a good night in bed is wi' a hot water bottle.'

'Ah huvnae heard o' wan o' they things fur years.'

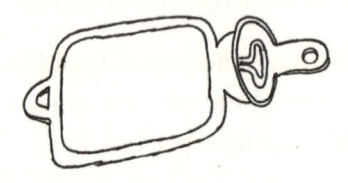

Two men

'Ma grandfather, a really super guy, left this mortal coil last year. He wis nearly 90. Great to be fit to the end. Well, to be honest, he actually staggered aff this mortal coil straight under a bus.'

Two women

'He's not really bad lookin' but in some lights maybe looks like Peppa Pig.'

'Jings. That's no' much o' a compliment. Does he grunt a lot?'

Group of men

'How many Covid jags have you had?'

'Ah think it's six.'

'Six. Ah've only had four. It's no' fair.'

'Ah can tell it's needlin' ye, mate!'

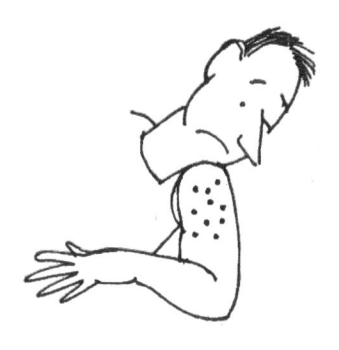

Group of women

'If you ask me, he's been training tae be a drunk fur years. Noo goat a first-class honours in it.'

Group of girls discussing pop stars

'Personally, I have no reason to dislike Taylor Swift. Well, Ah do really. She can sing and she's loaded.'

Two young women

'We found out Ah'm going tae have a girl. It's really exciting.'

'Have ye picked a name yet?'

'No. The names I suggest he doesnae like because he knows people he cannae stand wi' that name.'

Two women

'See when the TV announcer says that the following programme contains scenes which may upset some viewers, it jist makes me want tae watch it.'

Two women

'Knows every pub in Glesca like the back o' his hand. If they gave oot loyalty cards, it wid save him a fortune.'

Three women

'Ah prefer up the sterrs oan a double-decker. Ye can peer oot the windows at some o' the sights oan the streets.'

'I presume you are talking about some of our fine upstanding citizens!'

'Some o' them are no' capable of standing upright!'

Two women

'Oh, him? He couldnae come. He'll be in the bookies keepin' them in Rolls Royces.'

Two men

'See that Council we've goat. Well, Ah think they should call their meetings Fiddlers Rallies the way they keep putting up the rates. They're certainly no' in tune wi' the population.'

Two women

'That boy is bad tempered, ill-mannered and rude, jist like ma first husband. Anyway, he's deid noo. His new wife probably poisoned him.'

Two men

'She said Ah came home stotious. Ah didnae. Ah jist had a couple more than Ah normally have.'

Group of women

'Drugs is a bit o' a problem in oor area. Whit Ah say is them that take that stuff is haun-knitted dopes.'

Two young women

'How's yer brither?'

'Huh. Him! Ye can pick yer nose but no' yer family.'

Two women

'If you ask me, she's too young to be out with a man all night.'

'How old is your daughter now?'

'24.'

Two men

'She wis brought up in Bearsden so still thinks she's posh an' we're aw scruff. Probably voted fur Brexit jist tae come oot o' the Common Market.'

Luath Press Limited

committed to publishing well written books worth reading

LUATH PRESS takes its name from Robert Burns, whose little collie Luath (*Gael.*, swift or nimble) tripped up Jean Armour at a wedding and gave him the chance to speak to the woman who was to be his wife and the abiding love of his life. Burns called one of the 'Twa Dogs' Luath after Cuchullin's hunting dog in Ossian's *Fingal*. Luath Press was established in 1981 in the heart of Burns country, and is now based a few steps up the road from Burns' first lodgings on Edinburgh's Royal Mile. Luath offers you distinctive writing with a hint of unexpected pleasures.

Most bookshops in the UK, the US, Canada, Australia, New Zealand and parts of Europe, either carry our books in stock or can order them for you. To order direct from us, please send a £sterling cheque, postal order, international money order or your credit card details (number, address of cardholder and expiry date) to us at the address below. Please add post and packing as follows: UK – £1.00 per delivery address; overseas surface mail – £2.50 per delivery address; overseas airmail – £3.50 for the first book to each delivery address, plus £1.00 for each additional book by airmail to the same address. If your order is a gift, we will happily enclose your card or message at no extra charge.

Luath Press Limited
543/2 Castlehill
The Royal Mile
Edinburgh EH1 2ND
Scotland
Telephone: 0131 225 4326 (24 hours)
Email: sales@luath.co.uk
Website: www.luath.co.uk